The Western Front in Europe is the most vivid collective memory of the First World War, yet this was a global war, encompassing Russia, the Balkans, Italy, Mesopotamia and Palestine, great swathes of Africa, and the oceans. Moreover, it was a war of old and new forces: Britain's empire rallying to the 'mother country', America flexing its muscles to shift the balance of power. Old technologies were ranged alongside and against newer ones – horses and tanks, balloons and aeroplanes, sabres and machine guns, pigeons and radio.

In 1914, the war aim of all nations was simple: victory. In 19 celebrations, though hea muted. Too much had be war had left more proble solved. Even so, it would dismiss it as four years of meaningless slaughter. There was folly and suffering, but also courage, humanity and high ideals. Most of those caught up in the maelstrom believed theirs was a just cause. They deserve their memorials and the respect of later generations who remember them, and their Great War.

June Assassination of Austrian Archduke Franz Ferdinand at Sarajevo **August** War begins in Europe as Germany invades Belgium

Battle of Tannenberg: Russians defeated by Germans; German navy bombards east coast of England **September** First battle of the

British forces in France **December** Christmas truce in the trenches

In June 1914, two million British workers including builders, railwaymen, miners – and cricket-ball makers – were on strike. Suffragette leader Sylvia Pankhurst was arrested, for the eighth time. In London, theatre audiences applauded Mrs Patrick Campbell as Eliza Doolittle in Shaw's *Pygmalion* while, at Wimbledon, tennis fans followed the progress of Norman Brookes and Dorothea Chambers (singles champions that year). On 28 June, Austria's Archduke Franz Ferdinand was being driven with his wife through Sarajevo in Bosnia. Just before 11a.m. a student named Gavrilo Princip shot the royal couple. Nothing would ever be the same again.

The assassination of the heir to the Austro-Hungarian Empire precipitated a tit-for-tat slide into war. Austria sent an ultimatum demanding the Serbs submit to outside suppression of 'subversion'. British offers to mediate were snubbed, and the German Kaiser, Wilhelm II, seldom slow to anger, barked at Austria to stand firm. Europe's alliances closed ranks: Britain, France and Russia against the Central Powers: Germany and Austria-Hungary. King George V, the Kaiser and Tsar Nicholas II were cousins, but national honour outweighed family ties. The Anglo-German arms race was already well under way, ratcheted up in 1906 by the Royal Navy's first 'dreadnought' battleship. Britain suspected Germany's militarism, German colonial ambitions ('a place in the sun'), and German support for Irish nationalists seeking Home Rule.

ABOVE: King George V (right) rides with his German cousin, Kaiser Wilhem II, during a pre-war visit to Germany.

RIGHT: Archduke Franz Ferdinand and his wife Sophie progress to their car, and assassination, in Sarajevo. The killing of the heir to the Austro-Hungarian empire began the spiral into war.

TIMETABLE TO WAR

23 July	Austrian ultimatum to Serbia
25 July	Serbia's conciliatory reply is dismissed
26 July	Austria declares war on Serbia
30 July	Russia mobilizes to support the Serbs
31 July	Germany demands Russia halt mobilization
1 August	Germany declares war on Russia
2 August	Belgium refuses to let German troops cross its territory
3 August	Germany declares war on France
4 August	Germany invades Belgium. Britain declares war on Germany

LEFT: HMS *Dreadnought* (1906), a new breed of battleship, symbolized Britain's pre-war naval arms race, with Germany seen as the most threatening rival.

BELOW: Russian troops kneel in homage to their 'little father', Tsar Nicholas II. The First World War was destined to bring down the Romanov dynasty in Russia.

When Russia mobilized to back the Serbs, Berlin growled about a threat to Germany. Russia refused to back down. Germany declared war. France mobilized.

German strategy (the Schlieffen Plan of 1905) required a holding action against Russia, while German armies attacked France. To reach Paris, German troops must first cross neutral Belgium. By an 1839 treaty, a pact dismissed by the Kaiser as a 'scrap of paper', Britain was bound to defend Belgium. Diplomatic wires hummed; doors slammed, and as grey columns of German troops assembled on the Belgian frontier, Britain's Foreign Secretary, Sir Edward Grey, conjured an epitaph for an era: 'The lamps are going out all over Europe; we shall not see them lit again in our lifetime'. It was 3 August 1914. Next day, Britain was at war.

ALL OVER BY CHRISTMAS

War machinery was rusty, for none of the Great Powers had fought in Europe since the Franco-Prussian War of 1870–71. The Sarajevo assassination, successful only because the Archduke's driver took a wrong turning, precipitated a war that theorists had long planned, but for which armies were surprisingly unprepared. Despite Sir Edward Grey's pessimism, the British public were buoyantly jingoistic; bands played and crowds cheered soldiers off to the front. Even the Prime Minister was cheered in Parliament. 'Are we downhearted? No!' went the music hall song. 'It will all be over by Christmas' was the popular sentiment.

Lord Kitchener, war hero and now Secretary for War, pointed out that the British Expeditionary Force on its way to France had only 120,000 men. His call to arms produced five New Armies, totalling 2½ million men. Volunteers rushed to join what experts reckoned was the finest, and best-equipped, army Britain had ever sent to war. As the Germans smashed their way through Belgium, British 'Tommies' got their first taste of battle, at Mons (22–24 August 1914). Reports of 'heavenly visions' seen by the retreating troops made sensational headlines, and the 'Angel of Mons' became the first of many war myths.

Lord Kitchener makes his point.

BELOW: Men wait in the rain to join the army at a recruiting office in Whitehall, London.

‘YO

ARE T

I WA

Das Unterseeboot „U. 9" vernichtet 3 englische Panzerkreuzer

LEFT: An ominous overture, 22 September 1914. The German submarine U-9 sinks three British cruisers, and its skipper is celebrated in this German artist's impression.

The French piled in reinforcements (32 troop trains per day for a week). By September, 3½ million Frenchmen were in arms: 173 infantry regiments, 91 cavalry, 200-plus artillery units. The German sweep to encircle Paris was checked at the Marne (5–9 September), though at the cost of 238,000 French casualties. At Ypres in western Flanders (October–November), casualties topped 300,000, and 'Wipers' entered the British soldiers' vocabulary.

On the Eastern Front, as Austrian-Hungarian armies moved to crush the weaker Serbs, two Russian armies advanced into East Prussia (now within Poland). Russian hopes of speedy victory were dashed by defeat at Tannenberg in August 1914; two Russian generals, not speaking, allowed their armies to be split, and Samsonov's Second Army was annihilated. As winter set in, fronts 'solidified' like ground under frost. Trenches were dug, barbed wire strung and, as the troops shivered, the generals planned spring offensives. The war would not be over by Christmas.

THE TRUCE IN THE TRENCHES

On Christmas Day 1914, guns along stretches of the Western Front fell silent for a few hours. Some British and German soldiers left the trenches to shake hands, share cigarettes and brandy, and play football with bully-beef cans. Alfred Anderson of the Black Watch recalled the silence, broken by carols and greetings: 'We shouted "Merry Christmas", even though nobody felt merry.' By afternoon, the guns had opened up again.

LEFT: The machine gun was to prove a key weapon. Gas-masked gunners man a Vickers gun, a development of the Maxim first used in 1889.

ABOVE: The war gave new opportunities for advertisers. This poster, by Frank Dadd (1851–1929), reassured families that loved ones on the Western Front were nourished by home comforts.

French cavalry trotted to war in coloured uniforms, plumed helmets and gleaming breastplates, as they had at Waterloo in 1815. The British, having learned hard lessons in the South African war (1899–1902), wore khaki. Generals were confident cavalry could still win battles by galloping through gaps in the enemy lines; in reality a machine gun could decimate a cavalry squadron in seconds. As the infantry put on their new tin hats and dug for shelter in trenches and bunkers, the cavalry rode vainly in search of a role.

Gunners put their faith in artillery to break the deadlock; a French 75mm field gun fired 15 rounds a minute, and howitzers (heavy guns that lobbed shells onto the enemy) would flatten the hardest defences. Barrages of a thousand guns or more would demolish trenches, shred barbed wire, and demoralize any enemy soldiers not blown to pieces. Ahead of the barrage, infantry would walk forward to gain ground. The process would be repeated until the enemy gave up or were all dead. It seemed so simple.

German troops in 'coal scuttle' helmets and respirators seek out the enemy in the gas clouds.

1915

January First Zeppelin raids on Britain. **February** British fight off a Turkish attack on the Suez Canal. **March** Allied naval attack in the Dardanelles fails. **April** Start of Gallipoli campaign; first Battle of Ypres; first gas attacks on the Western Front. **May** Italy joins the war on the Allied side; the liner *Lusitania* is sunk by a German submarine. **August** Germans capture Warsaw from the Russians.

6

LEFT: British howitzers let fly at the enemy.

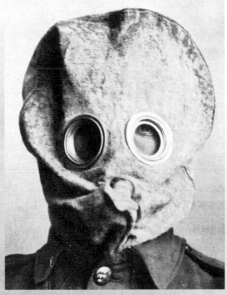

LEFT: Hooded warrior; a soldier peers out from an early gas mask.

The outcome was carnage for little gain. Artillery shells pounded fields and woods into grotesque, cratered desolation – but seldom eliminated entrenched defences. When infantry went 'over the top' into the open, they were scythed down by rifles and machine guns. The 'No Man's Land' between the opposing lines became a wasteland of shell holes, barbed wire, splintered trees, dead bodies, failed hopes.

Chemical warfare was tried at the second battle of Ypres (April 1915). From 5,700 canisters, the Germans released clouds of chlorine gas; 15,000 casualties resulted. At Loos (September 1915), the British retaliated but the wind changed, blowing their gas back on their own troops. Artillery gas shells delivered gas more effectively; in March 1918 on the Ypres San Quentin sector, German guns fired over 500,000 mustard gas shells. Hastily issued gas masks, or respirators, gave some protection to soldiers, who responded to this new horror with black humour and song: 'Gassed last night, and gassed the night before …'.

September Battles of Champagne and Loos on the Western Front. **October** Serbia collapses; Allies land troops in Salonika (Greece).
December Haig replaces French as commander of the British Expeditionary Force (on the Western Front)

7

ABOVE: Australians and New Zealanders aboard ship on their way to Gallipoli in 1915.

The Russian Empire mustered the First World War's biggest army of between 12 and 15 million, though most were poorly trained. Germany had 11 million soldiers, France more than 7.5 million, including thousands from colonies in Africa and Asia. British forces totalled 5 million, with about half the British Army overseas defending the British Empire.

The Empire sent millions of men to fight. The Indian Army alone numbered over half a million, and Indian troops fought on the Western Front, at Gallipoli, in the Middle East and East Africa. More than 50,000 African troops, recruited from British colonies, went into action, and thousands more served as non-combatants. South Africa contributed about 150,000 soldiers, led by the Boer generals Louis Botha and Jan Smuts. Caribbean islands sent around 21,000 men to war, most of whom came from Jamaica.

Australia, New Zealand and Canada all sent shiploads of volunteers, the Antipodeans earning a reputation for courage and toughness, notably at Gallipoli in 1915 but also on the Western Front. Their losses were disproportionately high –

ANZAC

The name ANZAC was first used in Egypt, where the combined Australian and New Zealand Army Corps, then 30,000 strong, was formed prior to the Gallipoli landings in 1915. After the heroism at Gallipoli, the first commemoration of ANZAC Day was in Brisbane in 1916, and the public holiday is observed in Australia and New Zealand on 25 April every year.

of 400,000 Australians, 59,000 were killed; of 110,000 New Zealanders, 18,000 died. Canadian troops first saw action at Ypres in 1915; their battle honours included the attack on Vimy Ridge (April 1917) during the battle of Arras. Of 600,000 Canadians who went to war, over 60,000 died.

Brief campaigns rolled up most of Germany's colonies. British and French troops attacked German Togoland and Cameroon (1914–16), and a South African force commanded by Botha captured German South West Africa (Namibia) in 1915. Japan (which went to war on 23 August 1914) helped the Allies occupy German Pacific outposts, such as the Caroline Islands; Australians captured German New Guinea, and New Zealanders took part in the occupation of German Samoa.

East Africa was a different story. There, for four years, a small German/African force (never more than 17,000 men), led by Paul von Lettow Vorbeck, defied 300,000 Allied troops. In a remarkable bush-fighting campaign, Lettow Vorbeck criss-crossed the continent, from Rwanda and Burundi to Tanganyika in the east, Northern Rhodesia and south to Mozambique. After surrendering on 25 November 1918, he returned to a hero's welcome in Germany.

BELOW: Indian troops man a Hotchkiss machine gun in France.

Troops from the British colony of the Gold Coast (now Ghana), during the campaign in German Togoland and Cameroon in 1914.

GALLIPOLI

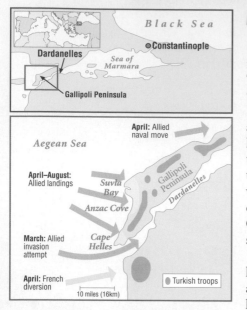

ABOVE: This map shows the Allied landings at the western end of the Gallipoli peninsula April 1915–January 1916.

The Ottoman Empire (Turkey) joined the Central Powers, opening up a new battlefront. In 1914, the German warships *Goeben* and *Breslau,* stationed in the Mediterranean, evaded Allied pursuit and were handed over to the Turks. Under German command, they shelled Russian ports on the Black Sea, provoking Russia to declare war on Turkey.

The Turks closed the Dardanelles strait linking the Aegean and the Sea of Marmara – Russia's only all-year ice-free sea link to its allies. In February 1915, Winston Churchill (at the Admiralty) proposed a naval attack to reopen the strait, threaten Constantinople, and perhaps force Turkey out of the war. British and French warships steamed into the narrow channel, which was mined and defended by Turkish forts firing German-made guns. The result was a disaster: three ships were sunk, and others badly damaged.

The Allies decided to occupy the Gallipoli peninsula to knock out the forts. On 25 April 1915, 75,000 Allied troops – about half of them Australians and New Zealanders – began landing at Cape Helles and at Gaba Tepe, later called Anzac Cove. Men landed from a collier-turned-landing craft, the *River Clyde,* and captured the fort at Seddul Bahr, but Allied forces were soon pinned down close to the beaches by heavy Turkish fire.

BELOW: Suvla Bay, Gallipoli. Men, horses and supplies poured in to the Allied beachhead.

In August, in a bid to cut off the peninsula, the Allies landed fresh divisions in the north at Suvla Bay. Again little progress was made. Casualties rose steadily. Sickness (especially dysentery) and a dispiriting lack of organization and weaponry added to the misery. The Allied troops at Gallipoli fought on gallantly into bitter winter weather, until the order came to withdraw. The last men were evacuated in January 1916.

The cost of Gallipoli was heavy in men and in reputations: British dead numbered over 40,000; ANZAC over 10,000; French around 8,000. The Turks lost as many as 65,000 men. General Sir Ian Hamilton, removed in October, received no further command; Churchill resigned from the Admiralty and went to fight in France. Gallipoli passed into legend: a military failure but a triumph of endurance and the 'ANZAC spirit'.

BELOW: Royal Navy warships in the Dardanelles, July 1915. The destroyer HMS *Raccoon* (foreground) has been hit by a Turkish shell.

BELOW: At Gallipoli, men made themselves as comfortable, and safe, as they could in makeshift bunkers that took on the appearance of shanty towns.

SIMPSON AND HIS DONKEY

This pair became part of ANZAC mythology. John Simpson Kirkpatrick enlisted to get home to England from Australia, but found himself at Anzac Cove, where he brought wounded men down from the front line on a donkey named Duffy. After four weeks, 'Simpson' was killed. Duffy was just one of thousands of animals that went to war. By 1917, the British Army had over 500,000 horses and 230,000 mules, and was buying 15,000 animals a month to replace losses.

RIGHT: Posters aimed straight at the conscience. Before 1916, men of fighting age still had the choice: to volunteer or not.

The British Army expanded rapidly after Kitchener's call to arms in 1914. A suggestion that friends would more willingly join up together led to the recruitment of the Stockbrokers' Battalion, formed in one week of August 1914 by London office workers. The name 'Pals' was given to these units by Lord Derby, who formed the Liverpool Pals, 1,500 men enlisting on the first day of the war (28 August). Tram drivers, ex-public schoolboys, footballers and friends from cities and towns, workplaces and clubs across Britain became 'pals' in uniform.

Such was the optimistic patriotism with which millions in Britain responded to Kitchener's call: 'Your country needs you …'. Peace campaigners and conscientious objectors voiced doubts and fears, but stirring war-speeches, rousing songs and conscience-pricking posters drowned out their protests. Lurid propaganda portrayed ravening Huns bayoneting babies and raping nuns. It became a matter of honour to fight: 'We don't want to lose you but we think you ought to go ...' urged a popular song. Few younger men out of uniform relished being looked on as a 'shirker' or branded a coward by being offered a white feather by a woman in the street. Most signed up eagerly and marched off, waving to friends and proud, if tearful, families.

Daddy, what did YO

BELOW: Leeds Pals at the battalion training camp in the Yorkshire Dales, September 1914.

in the Great War?

ABOVE: Labour politician
James Keir Hardie speaks
against the war in Trafalgar
Square, London.

The grim realities of trench warfare darkened the national mood. Though censors blue-pencilled bad news, and newsreel films usually showed 'the enemy' either dead or fled, the horrors of the Western Front were revealed. People were shocked by the ever-lengthening casualty lists and the appalling stories told by survivors – when persuaded to talk about their experiences.

Today, our view of the war is shaped not only by historians, but by war archives, letters and diaries, images and recordings. There are, too, the words of the war poets: among them Rupert Brooke, who died from blood poisoning on the Greek island of Skyros in 1915; Edward Thomas, killed in France in 1917; and Wilfred Owen, killed in France a week before the armistice in 1918. Like Nurse Edith Cavell, the poets suggest that 'patriotism is not enough'.

EDITH CAVELL

Matron of a Red Cross hospital in Brussels from 1907, Edith Cavell (born 1865), stayed at her post when Belgium was invaded. For helping Allied soldiers escape into neutral Holland, she was sentenced to death by a German military court, and shot on 12 October 1915. To the chaplain before her execution, she said, 'Standing as I do, in the view of God and eternity, I realize that patriotism is not enough. I must have no hatred or bitterness towards anyone.'

Royal Navy battle-cruisers steam into battle at Jutland, led by HMS *Lion*. Admiral Beatty's ship was saved by the gallantry of a gun commander and his men, who shut themselves inside their burning gun turret, and flooded it to prevent cordite explosive blowing the ship apart.

In Aid of the "JACK CORNWELL" WARD at the Star & Garter Home

ABOVE: Boy sailor Jack Cornwell (1900–1916), who fought at Jutland on HMS *Chester*, was (at 16) the youngest-ever winner of the Victoria Cross. He was wounded early on in the battle, but stayed at his gun post. He died in hospital in England.

I n 1914, with 42 battleships and battle-cruisers, the Royal Navy surpassed the German fleet (27). Britain also had the world's biggest merchant fleet, and a worldwide network of coaling stations. To offset this disadvantage, Germany planned to use mines, submarines and surface raiders to cripple British trade. In response, the Royal Navy was ordered to seize German merchant ships, blockade German ports and stop neutral ships on the high seas. By agreement, France kept its fleet in the Mediterranean, leaving the Atlantic and North Sea to the British.

British admirals waited their chance to take on the German fleet. The war began promisingly, with a daring attack on German warships in the Heligoland Bight (28 August 1914). Then came a shock defeat in the Pacific, when Admiral von Spee's squadron outgunned elderly British ships at the battle of Coronel (1 November 1914). Revenge was swift. In December, Admiral Sturdee's force, including the powerful battle-cruisers *Inflexible* and *Invincible*, destroyed the German squadron at the battle of the Falklands. A North Sea cruiser battle at the Dogger Bank (24 January 1915) was less conclusive.

1916

January Parliament votes for conscription. **February** Germans attack French fortress of Verdun. **April** Easter Rising in Ireland.
May/June Battle of Jutland between British and German fleets (31 May–1 June). **July** Battle of the Somme begins on the Western Front.

14

With naval aviation just beginning, the submarine was the most threatening new naval weapon. On 22 September 1914 the British lost three cruisers (*Aboukir*, *Hogue* and *Cressy*) to a single U-boat. However, unrestricted German attacks, such as that on the liner *Lusitania*, torpedoed in May 1915, were public relations disasters: 128 of 1,198 passengers who died were US citizens. Unescorted merchant ships fared badly: in 1917 over 2,400 Allied ships were sunk. Losses were stemmed only after the Allies organized convoys with destroyer escorts.

The Navy's 'big battle' came in the North Sea off Jutland, on 31 May 1916. In mist, smoke and gathering darkness, neither fleet was sure where the other was; at one point, British and German battleships were steaming in opposite directions. German gunnery proved superior. Three British battle-cruisers blew up, thin armour penetrated by plunging shells; *Indefatigable* was gone within 30 seconds, all but two of her 1,019 crewmen killed. Germany lost fewer ships (11 as against 14) and men (2,545 to 6,274). However, after Jutland, the German Navy did not risk battle again.

Q-SHIPS

Q-ships were decoys: disguised merchant vessels armed with hidden guns and anti-submarine devices. When a U-boat surfaced for the kill, the apparently helpless ship opened fire. Q-ships claimed at least 15 German submarines. Lt. Com. Gordon Campbell, in Q-ships *Farnborough* and *Pargust*, sank three U-boats, and was awarded the VC in 1917 for a successful 'kill' after his own ship was torpedoed.

Q-ship, the brigantine *Mary Y.*

LEFT: Newspapers and magazines illustrated the sinking of the Cunard liner *Lusitania*, torpedoed off Ireland on 7 May 1915 by the German submarine U-20.

August Hindenburg replaces Falkenhayn as German army chief in the West, after the German failure at Verdun. December Lloyd George succeeds Asquith as Prime Minister; Joffre is retired as commander of French forces.

MUD, BLOOD AND HEROES

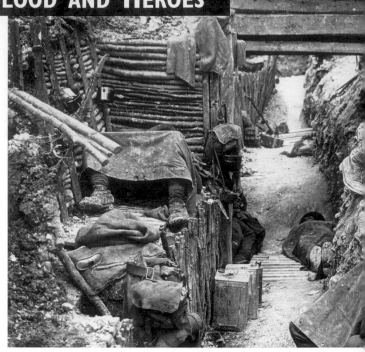

On the Western Front, the British Army put its faith in 'big guns'. Douglas Haig (in command from 1915) talked of 'flattening out the enemy's strongpoints'. German strategy also relied on artillery – to grind up the enemy in a 'mincing machine'. At Neuve Chapelle (March 1916), the British fired more shells in 35 minutes than in the entire South African War.

For much of 1916, the Germans attacked the French fortress-town of Verdun, hoping to draw more and more French troops into the mincer. Casualties on both sides topped 600,000, but (then) General Pétain's defence made him a French national hero. Britain was mourning one of its army heroes, Lord Kitchener, drowned on 5 June when his ship went down on its way to Russia.

The Allies planned a joint attack along the River Somme, but French losses at Verdun turned it into a mainly British operation. On 1 July 1916, after 3,000 guns had shelled enemy lines day and night for a week, 750,000 men of the British Fourth Army attacked on an 18-mile (30-kilometre) front. Some kicked footballs towards the enemy lines. Others walked confidently forward, expecting few, if any, German defences. But the artillery barrage had failed; German dugouts were intact.

ABOVE: A Mark I tank at the Somme. The tail wheel was for steering, the wire cage on top was to deflect bombs and grenades. Colonel Ernest Swinton was inspired to develop an armoured fighting vehicle by the American Holt tractor, which used a track system invented by Hornsby of Grantham in 1908. The result was the 'tank', a codename that stuck.

TOP: Dead and exhausted British soldiers in a trench on the Somme.

LEFT: Empty shell cases pile up after the Allied artillery barrage that opened the battle of the Somme in 1916.

TOP RIGHT: A map of the Western Front.

English Channel

NETHERLANDS

Ostend
Zeebrugge
Dunkirk
BELGIUM
Brussels
Calais
Ypres
FLANDERS
Passchendaele
Armentieres
Lille
Neuve-Chapelle
Loos
Mons
Vimy
Arras
Cambrai
R. Sambre
Peronne
R. Somme
St Quentin
Sedan
LUXEMBOURG
R. Oise
R. Aisne
R. Meuse
Verdun
Paris
St Mihiel
R. Seine
R. Marne
FRANCE

GERMANY

→ German offensives 1914
Deepest German penetration September 1914
▪ ▪ ▪ ▪ Front at beginning of 1915

Around 19,000 British troops were killed on a calamitous first day. Fifty of the new 'tanks' lurched into the battle, but half broke down. The battle dragged on until November, long after it was clear the breakthrough was not coming. British and Empire casualties were around 420,000, with 125,000 dead. French casualties were about half that; German the same if not more. The stalemate was unbroken. In the trenches, human resilience defied unimaginable miseries: wet, cold, smells, rotting corpses, rats, lice, trench fever, trench foot, constant shell and sniper fire. Yet morale and discipline held. During the war, 306 soldiers were shot by firing squads for offences including desertion and 'cowardice'; some were victims of 'shell-shock' which caused mental confusion, panic, even paralysis. A few days' rest was judged sufficient to restore all but the seriously wounded to fighting fitness. Then it was back in the line, for the next 'big push'.

ABOVE: Coiffure in the trenches. Cartoons by Bruce Bairnsfather (1888–1959) featuring 'Old Bill' are classics of wartime humour. The caption to this one read: 'Keep yer 'ead still or I'll 'ave yer blinkin' ear off'.

MINE AND COUNTER-MINE

Beneath the trenches was a secret tunnelling war between sappers burrowing up to 50 feet (15 metres) underground. Their goal was to place mines to destroy enemy trenches. The diggers, many of them peacetime coal miners, used stethoscopes to listen for sounds of digging from the other side; if telltale scraping was heard, they burrowed to intercept and blow in the enemy tunnel.

Italy joined the Allies in 1915. General Cadorna fought a series of gruelling battles along the Isonzo River in northern Italy against Austrian and German troops. After heavy defeat at Caporetto (October 1917), Cadorna was replaced by General Diaz, and the Italians dug in along the River Piave, resuming their advance in 1918.

In the Balkans, Serbia collapsed under attacks from Austria-Hungary, Germany and Bulgaria. Montenegro and Albania also fell. Some Serbian troops were evacuated to Corfu and joined an Allied landing at Salonika (Greece) in October 1915, though this came too late to save their country.

Serbia's traditional ally, Russia, was almost spent. General Brusilov launched the last big Russian offensive in June 1916; it cost a million Russian casualties. Its only real gain was to encourage Romania to declare war on Austria-Hungary in August 1916, but the Romanians were soon in retreat, and Russia started to crack apart, riven by revolutionary unrest.

Russia's old foe Turkey was led by radicals like Enver Pasha, a 'Young Turk' who welcomed German aid and German generals. Turkey had a capable army, but was beset by internal stresses fracturing the ramshackle Ottoman Empire. Mesopotamia (modern Iraq) was part of it, and there the British had occupied Basra (November 1914) to secure the Gulf oil fields. Heading north for Baghdad, General Townshend's force was besieged by the Turks at Kut el Amara, surrendering after four months (29 April 1916). Fewer than half the 10,000 British and Indians taken prisoner survived. Kut was recaptured in February 1917, and in March the British finally took Baghdad.

Turkish troops attacked the Suez Canal in 1915, but were repulsed by the British, who advanced through Sinai into Palestine. In the deserts of Arabia, T.E. Lawrence and the Hashemite ruler Husayn ibn Ali raised an Arab revolt against the Turks. Lawrence's Arab army captured the Red Sea port of Aqaba in July 1917, and General Allenby entered Jerusalem on 9 December. By September 1918, the British and their Arab allies were in Damascus. Victory fanned the flames of Arab nationalism, and made Lawrence an enigmatic celebrity.

RIGHT: Soldiers take cover, while Lewis gunners take on a German aircraft attacking these Indian troops in Palestine.

FAR RIGHT TOP: Gun crews and their horses pause during the Allied expedition to Salonika.

FAR RIGHT BOTTOM: Allenby walks into Jerusalem in 1917. A dismounted entry was suggested as a mark of respect to the Holy City.

OPPOSITE (MAIN): Alpine warfare called for strong legs, stout lungs and steady nerves. Italian troops on a mountain track in 1916.

LAWRENCE OF ARABIA

T.E. Lawrence (born 1888) was an Oriental scholar, traveller and archaeologist. In 1916, he was sent to organize an Arab revolt against Turkish rule. Lawrence raised a guerrilla army, and gave strong support to Husayn's son Faisal (later King of Iraq). After the war, hopes of a unified Arab nation dashed by the 1918 peace conference, Lawrence returned to Britain. To escape public attention, he changed his name first to Ross and then to Shaw, and joined the RAF. He died in a motorcycle accident in 1935.

Lawrence in the Bedouin dress he adopted for the desert.

19

KNIGHTS OF THE AIR

BELOW: In dogfights over the Western Front, aircraft twisted and turned in a deadly aerial ballet.

Air warfare was in its infancy in August 1914 as four squadrons of the Royal Flying Corps (RFC) flew to France. It grew fast, from reconnaissance to strategic bombing, with a battle for air supremacy over the Western Front. Fighter combats produced the first air aces, hailed by the press as 'knights of the air'.

The slow and flimsy 'scouts' of 1914 gave way to fighters twisting and turning at 130mph (210kph) and climbing to 20,000 feet (6,000 metres). At first, when their only weapons were revolvers, opposing pilots often waved to each other, but chivalrous skirmishing soon evolved into aerial 'dogfights', in which German Fokkers and British Sopwiths spat bullets from twin machine guns.

FIGHTER ACES

The war's most famous pilot was Manfred von Richthofen, known as the Red Baron because of the scarlet Fokker triplane he flew from 1917. Richthofen accounted for 80 Allied pilots before his death on 21 April 1918. He liked the aerobatic triplane because it could 'stand on its tail', allowing him to shoot an opponent from below. Other air aces included Frenchman René Fonck (75 victories), Britain's Edward 'Mickey' Mannock (73) and Canadian Billy Bishop VC (72). No pilot wore a parachute.

LEFT: The German Gotha bomber could carry a bomb load of 500kg (1,100lb). Its main weakness was a tendency to crash on landing. Oxygen was carried for the crew to breathe, as the planes flew as high as 6,000 metres (20,000 feet).

Bombing made a slow start. In September 1914, an RFC pilot dropped two bombs on German cavalry and a biplane of the Royal Naval Air Service (RNAS) bombed a Dusseldorf airship shed. The first German air raids came early in 1915, when Zeppelin airships attacked King's Lynn and Great Yarmouth. In May that year the first raid on London killed seven people, but 71 died in a five-Zeppelin attack of October. Slow and vulnerable, airships soon switched to night raids, the last of 51 attacks on Britain coming in April 1918; the airship raids killed 557 people.

Bombing aeroplanes were slow (under 100mph; 161kph), uncomfortable and cold for crews sitting in open cockpits. In the first German plane raid on London (28 November 1916), six bombs fell around Victoria Station. Larger aircraft meant greater destructive power. In London's worst raid, in June 1917, German Gotha bombers killed 162 people. Barrage balloons, anti-aircraft guns and nightly anxiety were a foretaste of the Blitz on Britain in 1940–41. In all, German air raids killed 1,413 civilians and wounded 3,409. British raids on Germany, which began in October 1917 using DH4 aircraft, killed 740 people and wounded 1,900. The armistice forestalled plans to bomb Berlin.

On 1 April 1918 the RFC and the RNAS were merged, creating the Royal Air Force. By the war's end, aviation was potentially the most decisive factor in strategy. In 1914 Britain had only 63 military aircraft; in 1918 there were over 22,000 in RAF service.

LEFT: Gordon Crosby's painting of the last moments of Zeppelin LZ37, shot down on 7 June 1915 by Sub Flight Lieutenant R. A. J. Warneford of No. 1 Squadron, Royal Naval Air Service. Warneford was awarded the Victoria Cross, but was killed in a flying accident 10 days later.

March Tsar Nicholas II of Russia abdicates. **April** USA declares war on Germany (6 April); mutinies in the French army on the Western Front. **June** First US troops land in France. **August** Passchendaele (third Battle of Ypres). **October** Communist revolution in Russia; Italians are defeated at Caporetto. **December** The British capture Jerusalem; Germany and Russia agree an armistice.

RIGHT: Women workers in the Royal Arsenal at Woolwich turn out bullets to keep the rifles firing.

The Home Front was a new battleground. From February 1916, single men and childless widowers aged 18 to 41 were conscripted into the forces. The resulting labour shortage saw a flood of women take on new jobs. More than 250,000 joined the Women's Land Army and the Women's Forage Corps to work on farms. 'Daylight saving' in 1916 brought them an extra hour in the fields. Many were already used to hard physical labour – in factories, fish docks and collieries – but faced new hazards in munitions plants, where toxic chemicals turned their skin yellow.

BELOW: This Women's Land Army poster urged women to harvest for victory.

For
FOOD PRODUCTION
FORAGE & TIMBER
The help of British Women
is urgent and indispensable

Recruits required
immediately for the

WOMEN'S
LAND ARMY

ENROL TO·DAY

Full particulars & application form
at nearest Employment Exchange
ASK AT POST OFFICE for ADDRESS.

Thousands more took paid jobs for the first time, or volunteered for organizations such as the First Aid Nursing Yeomanry, the Women's Legion and the Women's Emergency Corps (which taught middle-class ladies Morse code). Women ran offices, staffed shops, drove trams, buses and ambulances, delivered mail, served tea to soldiers. Regular army and navy nurses were joined by Voluntary Aid Detachments. Some worked close to the front line, in hospitals and casualty stations in France.

Women became police officers for the first time. Others joined the Women's Army Auxiliary Corps and the Women's Royal Naval Service (both founded in 1917). For their contribution to the war effort, the right to vote was unarguably a fair reward, though all women did not achieve this until 1928. Children's reward for doing their bit was to see Parliament

ABOVE: Air-raid damage in King's Lynn, Norfolk, after a raid by German naval airships in January 1915.

BELOW: A volunteer driver hoses down her ambulance (a converted Wolseley) in Cambridge, 1915.

raise the school-leaving age to 14. As submarine attacks on food convoys intensified, there was some belt-tightening, though few Britons went hungry. Families were encouraged to keep chickens and to grow vegetables. The government took over 2.5 million acres of land for agriculture. Prices rose: by Christmas 1916 a loaf of bread cost tenpence (roughly 4p). Food rationing (sugar, meat, margarine, butter and cheese) was introduced in 1917, and two 'meatless days' a week became the norm in smart London restaurants. Pub opening hours were cut to 5½ hours a day in 1915, and in 1917 the government nationalized Carlisle's breweries and pubs to cut drunkenness (Britain's biggest munitions plant lay nearby). To keep the Navy fuelled, coal mines were nationalized in 1914 (until 1921), and domestic coal was rationed in 1916.

SONGS OF THE WAR

The First World War left a rich legacy of hummable popular songs. Many were sentimental: *Roses of Picardy, If You Were the Only Girl in the World, Keep the Home Fires Burning*. Some entered the military repertoire, such as *Pack Up Your Troubles* and *It's A Long Way to Tipperary*. *Take Me Back to Dear Old Blighty* echoed every fighting man's wish. Blighty, from a Hindi word *bilati* meaning 'foreign', meant Britain, and a 'Blighty one' (a non-fatal wound requiring treatment and recovery at home) meant the chance to enjoy home fires again, if only for a month or two before returning to the Front.

RIGHT: 'The Kaiser sows his lies'; a French cartoon (1915). The German Emperor was usually portrayed by the Allied media as a megalomaniac, despite being a grandson of Queen Victoria.

BELOW: Carrier pigeons are shut up for protection against gas attack.

Before the war, newspapers and novels had aroused public fears of German spies plotting to sabotage the Royal Navy or to ship guns to Irish rebels. In this atmosphere of spy-mania, some trigger-happy patriots shot homing pigeons, in case they carried messages from enemy agents. The British Secret Service and Special Branch quickly rounded up a small group of German agents. The first to be executed was Carl Lody, a naval officer, shot in the Tower of London in November 1914. Among the intelligence he had sent to Germany was a (false) report that Russian troops had landed in Scotland to bolster the British war effort.

Although thousands of Irish soldiers had joined the British Army, anxiety persisted that Germany might support an armed rising in Ireland, where the continuing issue of Home Rule had still not been resolved when war began. The Easter Rising of 1916 in Dublin threatened to be such an opportunity, but Germany proved unwilling to commit troops to Ireland. An Irish patriot and former British consul in Africa, Sir Roger Casement, had landed in Ireland from a German submarine a few days before, to counsel delay unless German aid was confirmed. He was arrested, convicted of treason, and hanged.

Having taken over the world's submarine cable networks in 1914, Britain could intercept German, and neutral, communications. Code-breakers also got hold of German code books – one from a German cruiser aground in the Baltic, another seized by the Australian navy, a third found in a trawler net. Staff in 'Room 40' at the Admiralty decoded German messages. The German high command went on using the compromised codes until 1917, despite evidence that troop and ship movements were known to the Allies almost before they took place.

While the secret war was waged by stealth, the propaganda war was public and virulent. Allegations of German atrocities sparked off rabid anti-German feeling, and people with 'German' names found themselves accused of being spies or saboteurs. In May 1915, the British government decided to intern all 'enemy aliens'. Anti-German feeling became so strong that, in July 1917, the royal family changed its name, from Saxe-Coburg-Gotha to Windsor.

LEFT: Carl Lody, a German naval officer, travelled Britain in 1914 using a false name. Arrested as a spy in Ireland, he was shot in the Tower of London.

BELOW LEFT: King George V and Queen Mary, with the Prince of Wales (back row, left) visit France in 1917, having become thoroughly British 'Windsors'.

MATA HARI

The most celebrated spy of the 1914–18 war was Dutch-born Margaretha Zelle, better known as Mata Hari, exotic dancer. Born in 1876, she had become a celebrity performer, with high-ranking lovers across Europe. The French first suspected she was in the pay of the Germans, then persuaded her to work for them, and finally arrested her in 1917. Mata Hari was found guilty of espionage, and shot by firing squad – an elegant figure in a black velvet cloak, felt hat and black kid gloves. Her guilt or otherwise remains a matter of controversy.

Germany hoped to keep America out of the war, but clumsy diplomacy and unrestricted submarine attacks (U-boats sank five US ships in March 1917) incensed public opinion there. Congress pushed President Woodrow Wilson into war on 6 April 1917. Backed by the might of American industry, thousands of US soldiers were soon in training for Europe. General John 'Black Jack' Pershing resolved that Americans 'over there' would fight and win their own battles, and not be ordered around by French and British generals.

The imminent arrival of US troops spurred the British and French to try once more for the 'breakthrough'. The new French wonder-general, Robert Nivelle, advertised his plans before his attack at Arras, begun 10 days after the US entered the war. It failed. With mutinies breaking out in the hard-hit French army, Nivelle's replacement, Pétain, went on the defensive, waiting for 'the Americans and tanks'.

ABOVE: General John J. Pershing (1860–1948), commander of US forces in Europe, advances on his allies as he lands in France on 27 June 1917. 'Black Jack' regarded French and British tactics as too defensive.

RIGHT: *Oppy Wood 1917*, a painting by John Nash (1893–1977). The shattered wood near Arras, in France, was the setting for an unsuccessful British attack in May 1917.

LEFT: Field Marshal Sir Douglas Haig (1861–1928) reviews Canadian troops in the summer of 1918. Haig led the British Expeditionary Force in France, from December 1915 until the war's end. He was given an earldom in 1919.

BELOW: Disorganization and dissent, rather than defeat, crippled Russia. Lenin returned from exile to lead the revolution; this Communist propaganda photograph shows him in Moscow in October 1917.

Haig tried to keep up the offensive, to relieve the pressure on the French. In June 1917, a huge explosion on the Messines Ridge, north of Armentières, heralded the latest British attack. Nineteen enormous mines blew up simultaneously and 3,000 guns unleashed 4.5 million shells. Once again, the effect was less than hoped, for late summer rain had turned the battlefield into a morass: this was Passchendaele (the third battle of Ypres). By November, five miles' gain had cost over 300,000 British casualties.

A gleam of hope came from the tanks, more than 300 of which rolled forward at Cambrai (20 November 1917). Gains were made, and more than 10,000 prisoners taken; but the advance petered out and within a week the British were back more or less where they started. The Allies were in a bad way. Russia was in a spiral of collapse: strikes, riots, street-fighting, mutinies, confusion after the abdication of Tsar Nicholas II in March 1917. Kerensky's government tottered, and Lenin returned from exile to lead the Bolshevik revolution. By October, Russia was out of Europe's war and into a civil war. As 1918 dawned, Germany summoned its reserves for one last effort in the West.

THE ZIMMERMAN TELEGRAM

The final straw for the US Congress was the revelation that Germany was inciting Mexico to attack the USA. The Mexicans were promised lost territory (including Texas), after a US defeat. German foreign minister Alfred Zimmerman sent a secret telegram, with the plan, to the German embassy in Mexico. It was decoded by the British and handed to the Americans. Such perfidy incensed the most diehard isolationist. Uncle Sam pointed his finger, and 93 million Americans went to war.

THE ELEVENTH HOUR

RIGHT: The armistice signing; the German delegation meets the Allies, led by Marshal Foch, in a railway carriage.

Hindenburg and Ludendorff, the German supreme commanders, knew the spring offensive of 1918 was their last throw. Six thousand guns opened fire as German armies advanced, hoping to cut through to the coast between Abbeville and Dunkirk, and even reach Paris. The offensive ran out of steam an hour's truck ride from the French capital. With Americans swelling their numbers and superiority in tanks, guns and planes, the Allies regained the upper hand. In July alone 300,000 US troops landed.

The counter-attack along the Somme in August, known as the battle of Amiens, proved decisive. Though many British tanks still broke down, the Germans lost 400 guns and 27,000 men (of whom 15,000 became prisoners). Thousands more were trapped in the St Mihiel salient by French and US attacks, in which 1,500 Allied aircraft demonstrated the impact of mass air-power. By October 1918, demoralized Germans were in exhausted retreat. After four years, the Western Front was at last becoming fluid.

BELOW: A German destroyer scuttled at Scapa Flow after the German Grand Fleet was handed over to Britain.

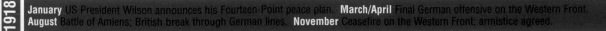

1918
January US President Wilson announces his Fourteen-Point peace plan. **March/April** Final German offensive on the Western Front. **August** Battle of Amiens; British break through German lines. **November** Ceasefire on the Western Front; armistice agreed.

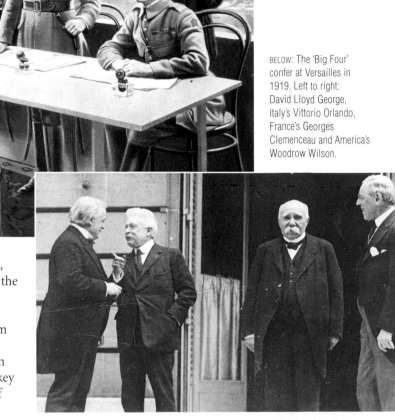

BELOW: The 'Big Four' confer at Versailles in 1919. Left to right: David Lloyd George, Italy's Vittorio Orlando, France's Georges Clemenceau and America's Woodrow Wilson.

In Germany, hunger, fuel shortages, street protests, talk of revolution, and the effects of a global influenza epidemic added to the misery of approaching winter. German sailors mutinied. From every front came bad news: Austria routed at Vittorio Veneto, its empire in meltdown; Bulgaria surrendered; Turkey beaten. The Kaiser bowed, Ludendorff was dismissed, peace overtures were made and an armistice was signed in a railway carriage in the forest of Compiègne, in France.

At 11a.m. on 11 November 1918, the guns stopped firing. The German High Seas Fleet steamed into the Firth of Forth, to surrender. It was over.

President Wilson hoped his Fourteen-Point plan would bring world peace, enforced by the new League of Nations, but the US Congress preferred isolation. The Treaty of Versailles of 28 June 1919 imposed harsh terms on Germany. The Allies' demand for reparations (compensation) left Germany drained, and in no doubt that it had lost the war. New nations arose from the dismantled Austro-Hungarian Empire (including Czechoslovakia, Yugoslavia and Hungary). Poland was reborn. The Ottoman Empire was consigned to history; it lost Mesopotamia (Iraq), Palestine and Syria, and a new Turkish Republic led by Mustafa Kemal Atatürk embarked on social revolution.

THE KAISER DEPARTS

Kaiser Wilhelm II left by car for exile in Holland, and on 28 November 1918 he abdicated – his chief of staff told him he should go, 'or shoot himself'. He died in 1941. Under the Versailles terms, Germany gave up Alsace-Lorraine to France and territory to Poland, Czechoslovakia and other states. The Rhineland was demilitarized. Germany also handed over 5,000 guns, 1,700 planes and 5,000 locomotives. At £6,600 million, reparations were set absurdly high and payment negotiations tottered on through the 1920s. By then the German currency had collapsed anyway.

December General election in Britain (28 December) returns the wartime coalition government led by Lloyd George; women vote for the first time (although it was not until 1928 that all women would be entitled to vote).

No 'War To End Wars'

TOP RIGHT: Soldiers sang 'When this lousy war is over . . .'. Now, at last, it was, and London celebrated en masse.

Old imperial rulers had gone: German Kaiser, Russian Tsar, Austrian emperor, Turkish sultan. But the green shoots of peace struggled to break through thick ashes of resentment, especially in Germany. With a worthless currency and a feeling that their army had been betrayed by the politicians, a growing number of Germans looked in despair for a saviour.

As fighting men came home to seek jobs, and understanding, a new decade shimmied in: the Roaring 20s, the 'jazz age'. But away from the bright lights were many homes without men, or with men whose bodies and minds were broken. Silent crowds stood in 1919 to mark Britain's new national day of remembrance, Armistice Day (11 November). King George V, adopting an idea born in Australia, called for a two-minute silence, so that 'the thoughts of everyone may be concentrated on reverent remembrance . . .'.

In 1920, the Unknown Warrior was entombed among the great in Westminster Abbey. On foreign battlefields great and small, war cemeteries were laid out, new gravestones replacing wooden crosses. Many soldiers had no known graves; a monument at Verdun records 150,000 such Frenchmen. R.C. Sherriff's play *Journey's End* and the novel *All Quiet on the Western Front* by Erich Maria Remarque both caught the public mood. Less serious were wartime adventure-yarns such as those of W.E. Johns' daredevil pilot, Biggles.

RIGHT: Solemn crowds in Whitehall observe Armistice Day, 11 November, at the Cenotaph.

The 1924 Empire Exhibition at Wembley, too, encouraged a hopeful spirit; but the Depression of the 1930s blew a bitter wind across the world. It took rearmament to put factories back in full production. In 1933, Adolf Hitler, a First World War soldier, became Chancellor of Germany, while Italy and Japan, both 'winners' in the 1914–18 war, became gripped by militaristic visions. All three countries ignored the ineffectual League of Nations. No wonder British and French politicians of the 1930s wore anxious expressions. Few could bear to contemplate another war. Too many scars were still unhealed. Yet as the 1930s drew on, people in Britain faced an awful truth: the First World War had not been 'the war to end wars'. Before long the world might be at war again.

THE HUMAN COST

Around 65 million combatants, mainly soldiers, fought in the First World War. More than 8 million of them were killed and 21 million wounded. As many as 13 million civilians died as a result of the fighting. Many millions more died in the post-war influenza epidemic. Military casualties (from combat and disease) for the leading nations were:

Britain/British Empire	908,000
France	1,356,000
Russia	1,700,000
Italy	650,000
United States	116,000
Germany	1,774,000
Austria Hungary	1,200,000
Turkey	325,000

ABOVE: Adolf Hitler (right) with fellow soldiers in 1914. He served with a Bavarian infantry regiment on the Western Front, and was twice wounded.

LEFT: The Tomb of the Unknown Warrior, near the west door of Westminster Abbey, London.

THE LEGACY OF WAR

ABOVE: Tyne Cot cemetery, between Passchendaele and Ypres in Belgium, is the largest war cemetery maintained by the Commonwealth War Graves Commission. Almost 12,000 Commonwealth soldiers killed between 1914 and 1918 are buried here.

The British Victory Medal bore the legend 'For Civilisation'. Wartime propaganda portrayed the First World War as a struggle for the rule of law against barbarism. In the aftermath, it seemed to many people that a better way of life had been swept away by the autumn gunfire of 1914.

Almost every town and village in Britain has its war memorial, and there are other smaller plaques and name boards in schools, town halls, stations, offices and factories. Here are listed those who 'gave their lives' in the Great War – a generation harvested by Death. As the last old soldiers have passed from life into history, their stories, preserved in archives, and in family photos and letters, are studied by a generation spared such horrors. Visitors to the huge war cemeteries in France and Flanders come away deeply moved by the sheer scale of loss, by the youth of so many of those who died.

Each year on Remembrance Day, the red poppies, imaging the flowers of the battlefields, and the silence, honour those who fought in the 1914–18 war, and their successors. Laurence Binyon's words have become their elegy. 'At the going down of the sun, and in the morning, we will remember them.'